To _____

From _____

Date _____

365 Things Every Dad Should Know

© 2005 Christian Art Gifts, RSA
       Christian Art Gifts Inc., IL, USA

First edition © 2005
Second edition © 2010

Compiled by Wilma le Roux and Lynette Douglas

Designed by Christian Art Gifts
Images used under license from Shutterstock.com

Printed in China

ISBN 978-1-77036-556-8

12 13 14 15 16 17 18 19 20 21 – 13 12 11 10 9 8 7 6 5 4

365 things every
DAD
should know

Contents

Foreword

Anyone can be a father, but it takes someone special to be a dad! There is nothing quite like having children to fill your life with unexpected pleasures and unusual experiences. Hearing what others say about their experiences sometimes helps to put yours in perspective.

This book combines wisdom, insight and a little humor to help you keep your sanity as your children grow toward adulthood. Enjoy it while you are tackling the adventure of that special father-child relationship.

Character, Example, and Integrity

1.

I know, my God,
that you test the heart
and are pleased with integrity.

1 Chronicles 29:17

2.

Count what is in a man,
not what is on him, if you would know
what he is worth – whether rich or poor.

Henry Ward Beecher

3.

How you react when the joke's on you
can reveal your character.

Robert Half

4.

This above all: to thine own self be true,
and it must follow as the night the day,
thou canst not then be false to any man.

William Shakespeare

5.

The man of integrity walks securely,
but he who takes crooked paths
will be found out.

Proverbs 10:9

6.

The greatest power for
good is the power of example.

7.

You don't raise heroes, you raise sons.
And if you treat them like sons,
they'll turn out to be heroes.

Walter M. Schirra

8.

A really intelligent man feels
what other men only know.

Baron de Montesquieu

9.

You can preach a better sermon
with your life than with your lips.

Oliver Goldsmith

10.

Jesus was gentle and meek, yet He was never weak or a soft touch. Follow His example as you father your children.

11.

The heart of every child beats to the rhythm of a father's love.

Steve Curley

12.

Happy homes are built with blocks of patience.

13.

If a child lives with encouragement, he learns to be self-confident.

14.

To set a lofty example is the richest bequest a man can leave behind him.

Samuel Smiles

15.

In everything set them an example
by doing what is good. In your
teaching show integrity.

Titus 2:7

16.

The first great gift we can bestow
on others is a good example.

Thomas Morell

17.

The words that a father speaks to his children in
the privacy of home are not heard by the
world, but, as in whispering-galleries, they are
clearly heard at the end and by posterity.

Jean Paul Richter

18.

Every father should remember that one day his
son will follow his example instead of his advice.

19.

We unconsciously imitate
what pleases us, and approximate
to the characters we most admire.

Christian Bovée

20.

There is only one way to bring
up a child in the way he should go
and that is to travel that way yourself.

Abraham Lincoln

21.

The Christian home is the Master's
workshop where the processes of
character-molding are silently, lovingly,
faithfully, and successfully carried on.

Richard Monckton Milnes

22.

How a man plays the game
shows something of his character;
how he loses shows all of it.

23.

A good example
is the best sermon.

Benjamin Franklin

24.

If you command wisely,
you'll be obeyed cheerfully.

Thomas Fuller

25.

He didn't tell me how to live; he
lived and let me watch him do it.

Clarence Budington Kelland

26.

The conscience of children is formed
by the influences that surround them;
their notions of good and evil are the result
of the moral atmosphere they breathe.

Jean Paul Richter

27.

One father is more than a
hundred schoolmasters.

George Herbert

28.

Children seldom misquote you ...
they repeat what you shouldn't
have said word for word.

29.

There are no real difficulties in a home where the
children hope to be like their parents one day.

William Lyon Phelps

30.

Give to us, Lord, a clear vision that we may
know where to stand and what to
stand for – because unless we stand
for something we shall fall for anything.

Peter Marshall

31.

Hate what is evil;
cling to what is good.

Romans 12:9

32.

Much good teaching can be nullified by the influence of a bad example. To teach right and live wrong is like feeding our children good food with one hand and poison with the other.

Dan S. Shipley

33.

You must be careful how you walk, and where you go, for there are those following you who will set their feet where yours are set.

Robert E. Lee

34.

Character building begins in our infancy and continues until death.

Eleanor Roosevelt

35.

The child becomes largely what it is
taught, hence we must watch what
we teach it, and how we live before it.

Jane Addams

36.

It is not fair to ask of others what you
are unwilling to do yourself.

Eleanor Roosevelt

37.

Children learn to deal with adversity
and triumph when they observe their
fathers remaining calm in the face of
one and humble in the face of the other.

Marriage
and Family Life

38.

Unless [our love and care for our family]
is a high priority, we will find
that we may gain the whole world
and lose our own children.

Michael Green

39.

A father and mother who present
a united front in matters of discipline
and order in the house provide
their children with a stable
environment that helps them
develop integrity and confidence.

40.

The tasks connected with the home
are the fundamental tasks of humanity.

Theodore Roosevelt

41.

Wives, submit to your husbands,
as is fitting in the Lord.
Husbands, love your wives
and do not be harsh with them.
Children, obey your parents in
everything, for this pleases the Lord.

Colossians 3:18-20

42.

Affection is responsible for nine-tenths
of whatever solid and durable
happiness there is in our lives.

C. S. Lewis

43.

House and riches are the inheritance of
fathers: and a prudent wife is from the LORD.

Proverbs 19:14 KJV

44.

The most significant relationship in the
family is by far that of husband and wife.
The quality of that relationship
truly governs the quality of family life.

Stephen Covey

45.

This is the true nature of home –
it is the place of peace;
the shelter, not only from injury,
but from all terror, doubt and division.

John Ruskin

46.

The goal of every married couple, indeed of
every Christian home, should be to make Christ
the Head, the Counselor, and the Guide.

Paul Sadler

47.

In the end only two things really matter
to a man, regardless of who he is;
and they are the affection and understanding
of his family. Anything and everything
else he creates is insubstantial.

Richard E. Byrd

48.

All the wealth in the world
cannot be compared with the happiness
of living together happily united.

Margaret d'Youville

49.

As a father has compassion
on his children, so the LORD
has compassion on those who fear Him.

Psalm 103:13

50.

Acceptance and appreciation tells the child that
he or she is of tremendous worth. And I can only
express my acceptance and appreciation through
being affectionate and available.

Josh McDowell

51.

The family was ordained by God before
He established any other institution,
even before He established the church.

Billy Graham

52.

If this world affords true happiness,
it is to be found in a home where love
and confidence increase with the years,
where the necessities of life come without
severe strain, where luxuries enter only
after their cost has been carefully considered.

A. Edward Newton

53.

The father of a righteous man has great joy;
he who has a wise son delights in him.

Proverbs 23:24

54.

The sanctity of marriage and the family relation
make the cornerstone of society and civilization.

James A. Garfield

55.

Accept one another,
then, just as Christ accepted you,
in order to bring praise to God.

Romans 15:7

56.

Life is made up, not of great sacrifices or duties,
but of little things, in which smiles and kindness
and small obligations, given habitually, are what
win and preserve the heart and secure comfort.

Sir Humphrey Davy

57.

The most important things we can give our kids
are our time, our lives, and our values – and
values are caught more than they are taught.

Tim Hansel

58.

By wisdom a house is built,
and through understanding
it is established.

Proverbs 24:3

59.

The most important thing a father can
do for his children is to love their mother.

Theodore Hesburgh

60.

Good family life is never
an accident but always an
achievement by those who share it.

James H. S. Bossard

61.

Strong families raise
strong, healthy children.

Alvin F. Poussaint

62.

A healthy family is sacred territory.

63.

Every house where love abides
and friendship is a guest, is
surely home, and home, sweet home;
for there the heart can rest.

Henry van Dyke

64.

If you are not willing to make time
for your children, then every other
piece of advice you get is meaningless.

Josh McDowell

65.

God sends children to enlarge our hearts;
and to make us unselfish and full of kindly
sympathies and affections; to give our souls
higher aims; to call out all our faculties to
extended enterprise and exertion; and
to bring round our firesides bright faces,
happy smiles, and tender loving hearts.

Mary Howitt

66.

A happy family is but an earlier heaven.

John Bowring

67.

Take Christ into your heart
and the life of your family, and
He will transform your home.

Billy Graham

68.

Enjoy one another and take the
time to enjoy family life together.
Quality time is no substitute for
quantity time. Quantity
time is quality time.

Billy Graham

69.

Your children need your presence
more than your presents.

Jesse Jackson

Work

70.

No worldly success can
compensate for
failure in the home.

David O. McKay

71.

The only place where success comes
before work is in the dictionary.

72.

All growth depends upon activity.
There is no development physically or
intellectually without effort, and effort
means work. Work is not a curse; it is the
prerogative of intelligence, the only means to
manhood, and the measure of civilization.

Calvin Coolidge

73.

A good character, good habits,
and iron industry are impregnable
to the assaults of all the ill luck
that fools ever dreamed of.

Joseph Addison

74.

It has been my observation
that most people get ahead
during the time that others waste.

Henry Ford

75.

One of the chief reasons for success in
life is the ability to maintain a daily
interest in one's work, to have a chronic
enthusiasm; to regard each day as important.

William Lyon Phelps

76.

There can be intemperance
in work just as there is in drink.

C. S. Lewis

77.

Unless each day can be looked upon
by an individual as one in which
he has had some fun, some joy,
some real satisfaction, that day is a loss.

Dwight Eisenhower

78.

Few people do business well
who do nothing else.

Lord Chesterfield

79.

Getting along with others
is the essence of getting ahead,
success being linked with cooperation.

William Feather

80.

Whatever you do,
work at it with all your heart,
as working for the Lord, not for men.

Colossians 3:23

81.

Men cannot labor on always.
They must have recreation.

Orville Dewey

82.

Whatever you do,
do it all for the glory of God.

1 Corinthians 10:31

83.

What is this world if, full of care,
we have no time to stand and stare?

W. H. Davies

84.

Remember: the one who wins
the rat race, is still a rat.

85.

You were intended not only to work,
but to rest, laugh, play and have proper leisure
and enjoyment. To develop an all-round
personality you must have interests outside
of your regular vocation that will serve to
balance your business responsibilities.

Grenville Kleiser

86.

Without rest, a man cannot
work; without work, the rest
does not give you any benefit.

Abkhasian Proverb

87.

The plans of the diligent
lead to profit as surely
as haste leads to poverty.

Proverbs 21:5

88.

The highest reward for a person's
toil is not what he gets for it,
but what he becomes by it.

John Ruskin

Faith and Believing

89.

These commandments that I give you today are to be upon your hearts. Impress them on your children. Talk about them when you sit at home and when you walk along the road, when you lie down and when you get up.

Deuteronomy 6:6-7

90.

But as for me and my household,
we will serve the Lord.

Joshua 24:15

91.

Just as your children have a father, you also have a Father – a perfect heavenly Father who sees to it that you are never alone.

92.

Where can I go from Your Spirit? Where can I flee from Your presence? If I go up to the heavens, You are there; if I make my bed in the depths, You are there. If I rise on the wings of the dawn, if I settle on the far side of the sea, even there Your hand will guide me, Your right hand will hold me fast.

Psalm 139:7-10

93.

Cast all your anxiety on Him
because He cares for you.

1 Peter 5:7

94.

The more a man bows his knee before God,
the straighter he stands before men.

95.

If you take being a father seriously, you'll
know that you're not big enough for the job,
not by yourself. Being a father will put you
on your knees if nothing else ever did.

Elisabeth Elliot

96.

A man without religion or spiritual
vision is like a captain who finds himself
in the midst of an uncharted sea, without
compass, rudder and steering wheel.
He never knows where he is, which way
he is going and where he is going to land.

William J. H. Boetcker

97.

The child of many prayers shall never perish.

An old Christian to St. Monica, mother of St. Augustine

98.

A Christian is the keyhole
through which other people see God.

Robert E. Gibson

99.

A child is not likely to find a Father in God,
unless he finds something of God in his father.

Austin L. Sorensen

100.

Pray together and read the Bible together.
Nothing strengthens a marriage and family more.
Nothing is better defense against Satan.

Billy Graham

101.

He who fears the LORD has a secure fortress,
and for his children it will be a refuge.

Proverbs 14:26

102.

Children miss nothing in sizing up their parents.
If you are only half convinced of your beliefs,
they will quickly discern that fact.

James Dobson

103.

A Christian father should be able to echo
the words of Paul, "Follow my example,
as I follow the example of Christ."

104.

We should speak to God from our own hearts,
and talk to Him as a child talks to a father.

Charles H. Spurgeon

105.

I have held many things in my hands, and
I have lost them all; but whatever I have
placed in God's hands, that I still possess.

Martin Luther

106.

Having knowledge of the Bible
is essential to a rich and meaningful life.

Billy Graham

107.

To worship is to quicken the conscience by the
holiness of God, to feed the mind with the truth
of God, to purge the imagination by the beauty of
God, to open the heart to the love of God,
to devote the purpose to the will of God.

William Temple

108.

"The family that prays together, stays together"
is much more than a cliché! And when the
family adds the dimension of praying together in
church, the truth becomes even stronger.

Zig Ziglar

109.

Come near to God and
He will come near to you.

James 4:8

110.

Anything that dims my vision for Christ,
or takes away my taste for Bible study,
or cramps me in my prayer life, or makes
Christian work difficult, is wrong for me;
and I must, as a Christian, turn away from it.

J. Wilbur Chapman

Love

111.

A child should be loved
for who he is, not for what he does.

David Jeremiah

112.

Spread love everywhere you go:
First of all in your own house ...
let no one ever come to you without
leaving better and happier. Be the
living expression of God's kindness;
kindness in your face, kindness in
your eyes, kindness in your smile,
kindness in your warm greeting.

Mother Teresa

113.

When you love someone,
you love him as he is.

Charles Peguy

114.

If a child lives with acceptance, he learns to love.

115.

Happiness is to be found only in the
home where God is loved and honored, where
each one loves and helps, and cares for others.

St. Theophane Venard

116.

[Love] always protects, always trusts,
always hopes, always perseveres.

1 Corinthians 13:7

117.

Follow the way of love.

1 Corinthians 14:1

118.

To love is to be vulnerable.

C. S. Lewis

119.

Every child knows that love is spelled: T-I-M-E.

120.

The heart of a child is the most precious
of God's creation. Never break it.
At all costs, never break it.

Joseph L. Whitten

121.

You will find, as you look back
upon your life, that the moments
when you really lived are the
moments when you have done
things in the spirit of love.

Henry Drummond

122.

A child needs your love most
when he deserves it least.

Erma Bombeck

123.

If a child lives with love, he learns
that the world is a wonderful place to live in.

124.

You aren't loved because you're valuable:
You're valuable because God loves you.

125.

Live a life of love, just as Christ loved us.

Ephesians 5:2

126.

You learn to love by loving.

Francis of Sales

127.

Your children may forget what you
have taught them, but they will never
forget how you made them feel.

Carl W. Buechner

128.

Love is a great teacher.

St. Augustine

129.

May the Lord make your love increase
and overflow for each other and for
everyone else, just as ours does for you.

1 Thessalonians 3:12

130.

When I have learned to love God better
than my earthly dearest, I shall love my
earthly dearest better than I do now.

C. S. Lewis

131.

Let love and faithfulness never leave
you; bind them around your neck,
write them on the tablet of your heart.

Proverbs 3:3

132.

To love another person
is to help them love God.

Søren Kierkegaard

133.

It is by loving and being loved that one
can come closest to the soul of another.

George MacDonald

134.

Man while he loves is never quite depraved.

Charles Lamb

Dads and Their Kids

135.

Some of the best things you can give
your children are good memories.

136.

Affirming words from moms and dads are like
light switches. Speak a word of affirmation at the
right moment in a child's life and it's like
lighting up a whole roomful of possibilities.

Gary Smalley

137.

Dad.
He dreams, he plans, he struggles
that we might have the best. His sacrifice
is quiet, his life is love expressed.

138.

The soul is healed by being with children.

Fyodor Dostoevsky

139.

The best way to advise your children is to
find out what they want, and then to let
them know how they can go about getting it.

Harry S. Truman

140.

If you can give your son or daughter
only one gift, let it be Enthusiasm.

Bruce Barton

141.

Children are likely to live up
to what their fathers believe of them.

Lady Bird Johnson

142.

People who really love each other
are the happiest people in the world.
They love their children
and they love their families.
They may have very little,
but they are happy.

Mother Teresa

143.

Give a little love to a child
and you get a great deal back.

John Ruskin

144.

See as a child sees –
the joy, the wonder, the hope.

145.

Encouragement is oxygen to the soul.

George M. Adams

146.

You can learn many things from children.
How much patience you have, for instance.

Franklin P. Jones

147.

If your children spend most
of their time in other people's houses,
you're lucky; if they all congregate
at your house, you're blessed.

148.

Nothing you do for your children is ever wasted.
They seem not to notice us, hovering, averting
our eyes, and they seldom offer thanks, but what
we do for them is never wasted.

Garrison Keillor

149.

When you thought I wasn't looking, I
heard you say "thank you" and I wanted
to say thanks for all the things I saw
when you thought I wasn't looking.

150.

Teenagers need you to be silent
and invisible, but very palpably *there*.

Laurie Graham

151.

Teenagers are people who
express a burning desire to be
different by dressing exactly alike.

152.

The potential possibilities of
any child are the most intriguing
and stimulating in all creation.

Ray L. Wilbur

153.

The more parents make eye contact with
their children as a means of expressing
their love, the more a child is nourished with
love and the fuller is his emotional tank.

Ross Campbell

154.

Every boy has the right to play
so that he may stretch the imagination
and prove his prowess and skill.

Herbert Hoover

155.

In the final analysis it is not what you do
for your children but what you have taught
them to do for themselves that will
make them successful human beings.

Ann Landers

156.

There is no such thing as a recipe
for raising children that works for all parents
and all children and in all circumstances.
Raising a child requires an awareness of
the uniqueness of each child and a loving
response to his distinctive personality.

Jörg Zinc

157.

God has sent children into the world,
not only to replenish it, but also to serve as
sacred reminders of something ineffably precious
which we are always in danger of losing.

Elton Trueblood

158.

How many hopes and fears,
how many ardent wishes and anxious
apprehensions are twisted together in the
threads that connect the parent with the child.

Samuel G. Goodrich

159.

There are many ways to measure success;
not the least of which is the way your
child describes you when talking to a friend.

160.

Kiss your kids goodnight every evening,
even if it wakes them up.

Bruce and Stan

161.

Don't help your child to accomplish
something that he can accomplish on his own.
Don't deny him the priceless privilege
and thrill of developing his own success.

Dale Carnegie

162.

I hope my son will remember me one
day not for the battles I won but
because I prayed with him each evening.

Douglas MacArthur

163.

A father is his child's protector,
confidant and tutor.

164.

Give your child room within the boundaries
of your trust to experiment and grow
into the man God created him to be.

165.

First seek to understand,
then to be understood.

Steven Covey

166.

My father never talked to me about how
to treat people. Every act of kindness
I have ever shown another person was
because I was trying to imitate him.

Pamela McGrew

167.

Before I got married I had six theories
about bringing up children; now
I have six children and no theories.

Lord Rochester

168.

The greatest gift I ever received was a gift
I got one Christmas when my dad gave me
a small box. Inside was a note saying, "Son, this
next year I will give you 365 hours, an hour every
day after dinner." My dad not only kept
his promise, but every year he renewed it
and it's the greatest gift I ever had in my life.

169.

If a man is fortunate he will, before he dies,
gather up as much as he can of his civilized
heritage and transmit it to his children.

Will Durant

170.

A baby has a way of making
a man out of his father,
and a boy out of his grandfather!

Angie Papadakis

171.

Praise is well, compliment is well,
but affection – that is the last and
most precious reward that any man can win,
whether by character or achievement.

Mark Twain

172.

The righteous man leads a blameless life;
blessed are his children after him.

Proverbs 20:7

173.

Only those who respect the personality
of others can be of real use to them.

Albert Schweitzer

174.

Your children are a mirror
which reflects back on you
the kind of image you cast.

Fulton Sheen

175.

He must manage his own family well and see
that his children obey him with proper respect.

1 Timothy 3:4

176.

What is important is not so much who
my father was but how I remember him.

Anne Sexton

177.

Never worry too much about the things
you can replace, worry only about
the things you can't replace.

Winnie Johnson

178.

We cannot form our children
on our own concepts; we must take them
and love them as God gives them to us.

Johann Wolfgang von Goethe

Stewardship

179.

Remember that money can't buy love.

180.

Filling a child's room with games
and toys and material things,
can never fill his heart with love.

181.

The easy way to teach children
the value of money
is to borrow from them.

182.

It is not what he has, or even
what he does which expresses
the worth of a man, but what he is.

Henri Frédéric Amiel

183.

Good will come to him who is generous and
lends freely, who conducts his affairs with justice.

Psalm 112:5

184.

Though your riches increase,
do not set your heart on them.

Psalm 62:10

185.

Better a dry crust with peace and quiet
than a house full of feasting, with strife.

Proverbs 17:1

186.

Save a part of your income and begin
now, for the man with a surplus controls
circumstances and the man without
a surplus is controlled by circumstances.

Henry H. Buckley

187.

A man who both spends and saves money is the
happiest man, because he has both enjoyments.

Samuel Johnson

188.
Ask thy purse what thou shouldst spend.
Scottish Proverb

189.
Children are the poor man's wealth.
Danish Proverb

190.
Honor the LORD with your wealth,
with the firstfruits of all your crops;
then your barns will be filled to overflowing,
and your vats will brim over with new wine.
Proverbs 3:9-10

191.
"What good is it for a man to gain the whole
world, yet forfeit his soul? Or what can a man
give in exchange for his soul?"
Mark 8:36-37

192.
In short, the way to wealth, if you
desire it, is as plain as the way to market.
It depends chiefly on two words,
industry and frugality; that is, waste neither
time nor money, but make the best use of both.
Benjamin Franklin

193.

"Do not store up for yourselves treasures on earth, where moth and rust destroy, and where thieves break in and steal. But store up for yourselves treasures in heaven, where moth and rust do not destroy, and where thieves do not break in and steal. For where your treasure is, there your heart will be also."

Matthew 6:19-21

194.

One man gives freely, yet gains even more; another withholds unduly, but comes to poverty.

Proverbs 11:24

195.

We can tell our values by looking at our checkbook stubs.

196.

There are but two ways of paying debt: increase of industry in raising income, increase of thrift in laying out.

Thomas Carlyle

197.

It isn't the big pleasures that count the most;
it's making a great deal out of the little ones.

Jean Webster

198.

Get all you can, without hurting your soul,
your body or your neighbor. Save all you can,
cutting off every needless expense. Give all
you can. Be glad to give, and ready to distribute;
laying up in store for yourselves a good
foundation against the time to come.

John Wesley

199.

The habit of saving is itself an education;
it fosters every virtue, teaches self-denial,
cultivates the sense of order, trains to
forethought, and so broadens the mind.

Thornton T. Munger

200.

A father is a banker provided by nature.

French Proverb

201.

But remember the LORD your God, for it is
He who gives you the ability to produce
wealth, and so confirms His covenant, which
He swore to your forefathers, as it is today.

Deuteronomy 8:18

202.

Let's not get so busy or live so fast
that we can't listen to the music
of the meadow or the symphony
that glorifies the forest. Some things
in the world are far more important
than wealth; one of them is the
ability to enjoy simple things.

Dale Carnegie

203.

I assume that you save and long for wealth
only as a means of enabling you the better
to do some good in your day and generation.

Andrew Carnegie

Training a Child

204.

Fathers, do not exasperate your children;
instead, bring them up in the training
and instruction of the Lord.

Ephesians 6:4

205.

Train a child in the way he should go,
and when he is old he will not turn from it.

Proverbs 22:6

206.

Praise your children openly, reprove them secretly.

W. Cecil

207.

To teach is to learn twice.

Joseph Joubert

208.

I have thought about it a great deal, and the more
I think, the more certain I am that obedience is
the gateway through which knowledge, yes, and
love, too, enter the mind of a child.

Annie Sullivan

209.

One thing scientists have discovered
is that often-praised children become more
intelligent than often-blamed ones.

Thomas Dreier

210.

When you lead your sons and daughters
in the good way, let your words
be tender and caressing, in terms
of discipline that wins the heart's assent.

Elijah Ben Solomon Zalman

211.

A refusal to correct is a refusal to love;
love your children by disciplining them.

Proverbs 13:24 THE MESSAGE

212.

Our fathers disciplined us for a little while
as they thought best; but God disciplines
us for our good, that we may share in His
holiness. No discipline seems pleasant
at the time, but painful. Later on, however,
it produces a harvest of righteousness and
peace for those who have been trained by it.

Hebrews 12:10-11

213.

Discipline your son, and he will give you
peace; he will bring delight to your soul.

Proverbs 29:17

214.

Every child should have an occasional pat
on the back, as long as it is applied
low enough and hard enough.

Bishop Fulton J. Sheen

215.

My son, do not despise the LORD's
discipline and do not resent His rebuke,
because the LORD disciplines those He loves,
as a father the son he delights in.

Proverbs 3:11-12

216.

If you desire the reformation and welfare of your
people, do all you can to promote family religion.

Richard Baxter

217.

Do not handicap your children
by making their lives easy.

Robert Heinlein

218.

Children can stand vast amounts of
sternness. It is injustice, inequity,
and inconsistency that kill them.

Father Robert Capon

219.

Discipline and love are not opposites,
one is a function of the other.

James Dobson

220.

When dealing with your child's wrongdoing,
remember the words of Augustine,
"Love the sinner but hate the sin."

221.

He that will have his son have respect
for him and his orders, must himself
have a great reverence for his son.

John Locke

222.

Criticism, like rain, should be gentle
enough to nourish a [child's] growth
without destroying his roots.

Frank A. Clark

223.

A man's feelings of goodwill
toward others is the strongest magnet
for drawing goodwill from others.

Lord Chesterfield

224.

When angry, count to ten before you speak;
if very angry, 100.

Thomas Jefferson

225.

A patient man has great understanding,
but a quick-tempered man displays folly.

Proverbs 14:29

226.

"Fit the punishment to the crime" is the surest
and fairest way to help a child understand
the consequences of his wrongdoing.

227.

If a child lives with criticism,
he learns to condemn. If a child lives with
hostility, he learns to fight. If a child lives
with ridicule, he learns to be shy. If a child
lives with fairness, he learns justice.

228.

One should not only serve youth but
should also avoid offending them by
word or deed. One should give them the
best of training that they may learn to pray.

Martin Luther

229.

A child educated only at
school is an uneducated child.

George Santyana

230.

Sometimes we must hurt in order to
grow, we must fail in order to know,
we must lose in order to gain,
some lessons are learned best
only through pain.

Achievements and Self-esteem

231.

Living and dreaming
are two different things – but
you can't do one without the other.

Malcolm Forbes

232.

If a child lives with encouragement,
he learns to be self-confident.

233.

There is no genius in life like
the genius of industry and energy.

Donald G. Mitchell

234.

Celebration is more than a happy feeling.
Celebration is an experience. It is liking others,
accepting others, laughing with others.

Douglas Stuva

235.

Life affords no greater pleasure
than overcoming obstacles.

236.

Said will be a little ahead,
but done should follow at his heel.

Charles H. Spurgeon

237.

My father gave me
the greatest gift anyone could give
another person, he believed in me.

Jim Valvano

238.

For though a righteous man
falls seven times, he rises
again, but the wicked are
brought down by calamity.

Proverbs 24:16

239.

To be successful, you've
got to be willing to fail.

Frank Tyger

240.

The secret of success is
constancy to purpose.

Benjamin Disraeli

241.

The more we do, the more we can do.

William Hazlitt

242.

We all stumble, every one of us. That's why
it's a comfort to go hand in hand.

Emily Kimbrough

243.

God has a wonderful plan for each person ...
He knew even before He created this world what
beauty He would bring forth from our lives.

Louis B. Wyly

244.

Fathers, do not embitter your children,
or they will become discouraged.

Colossians 3:21

245.

People rarely succeed unless
they have fun in what they are doing.

Dale Carnegie

246.

Failure is success if we learn from it.

Malcolm Forbes

247.

Far away in the sunshine are my highest aspirations. I may not reach them, but I can look up and see their beauty, believe in them, and try to follow where they lead.

Louisa May Alcott

248.

Wise men learn by other
men's mistakes, fools by their own.

H. G. Bohn

249.

God has given each of you some special abilities; be sure to use them to help each other, passing on to others God's many kinds of blessings.

1 Peter 4:10 TLB

250.

Never be lacking in zeal, but keep
your spiritual fervor, serving the lord.

Romans 12:11

251.

Many of life's failures are people
who did not realize how close
they were to success when they gave up.

Thomas Edison

252.

Allow your dreams a place in your prayers
and plans. God-given dreams can help you
move into the future He is preparing for you.

Barbara Johnson

253.

When we look for the good in others,
we discover the best in ourselves.

Martin Walsh

254.

God's various expressions of power are in
action everywhere; but God Himself is
behind it all. Each person is given something
to do that shows who God is: Everyone gets
in on it, everyone benefits. All kinds of things
are handed out by the Spirit, and to all
kinds of people! The variety is wonderful.

1 Corinthians 12:6-7 THE MESSAGE

255.

If a child lives with approval,
he learns to live with himself.

Dorothy Law Nolte

256.

Our greatest glory consists not in never
failing, but in rising every time we fall.

Oliver Goldsmith

257.

The praises of others may be
of use in teaching us not what we
are, but what we ought to be.

Augustus Hare

258.

Whatever crushes individualism is despotism,
by whatever name it may be called.

John Stuart Mill

259.

I have yet to find a man, whatever his situation in life, who did not do better work and put forth greater effort under a spirit of approval than he would ever do under a spirit of criticism.

Charles M. Schwab

260.

You have a unique message to deliver, a unique song to sing, a unique act of love to bestow. This message, this song, and this act of love have been entrusted exclusively to the one and only you.

John Powell

261.

Above all, love each other deeply, because love covers over a multitude of sins.

1 Peter 4:8

262.

Teach your children to use
what talents they have:
the woods would be silent if no
bird sang except those that sing best.

263.

Success comes in cans,
failure comes in can'ts.

264.

There is something very powerful
about someone believing in you,
someone giving you another chance.

Sheila Walsh

265.

The family should be a place
where each new human being
can have an early atmosphere conducive
to the development of constructive creativity.

Edith Schaeffer

266.

There is no verbal vitamin
more potent than praise.

Frederick B. Harris

267.

Most of us, swimming against tides
of trouble the world knows nothing
about, need only a bit of praise or
encouragement – and we'll make the goal.

Jerome P. Fleishman

268.

Life is not easy for any of us. But what of that?
We must have perseverance and, above all,
confidence in ourselves. We must believe that
we are gifted for something, and that this thing,
whatever the cost, must be attained.

Marie Curie

269.

Today's kids desperately need dads who
give the credit to others and empower those
they touch to succeed in all they do.

Marty Wilkins

270.

If you've had a good time playing the
game, you're a winner even if you lose.

Malcolm Forbes

Humor

271.

Today's kids desperately need dads
who laugh till their belly hurts and tears
fall from their eyes while secretly creating deep
friendships and memories that last a lifetime.

Marty Wilkins

272.

Of all the things God created,
I am often most grateful
He created laughter.

Charles R. Swindoll

273.

Where morning
dawns and evening fades
You call forth songs of joy.

Psalm 65:8

274.

Laughter is the key to surviving
the specific stress experienced during
the years of bringing up children.

James Dobson

275.

Whole-hearted, ready laughter heals,
encourages, relaxes anyone within hearing
distance. The laughter that springs
from love makes wide the space around –
gives room for the loved one to enter in.

Eugenia Price

276.

Laughing at ourselves as well
as with each other gives a
surprising sense of togetherness.

Hazel C. Lee

277.

I rejoice in life for its own sake. Life is no brief
candle for me. It is a sort of splendid torch,
which I have got hold of for the moment; and
I want to make it burn as brightly as possible
before handing it on to future generations.

George Bernard Shaw

278.

This is the day the LORD has made;
let us rejoice and be glad in it.

Psalm 118:24

279.

While walking on the taut rope over the
precipice of life, a sense of humor is the
staff with which we keep our balance.

Elsa Maxwell

280.

Good humor is a tonic for mind
and body. It is the best antidote
for anxiety and depression.

Garrison Keillor

281.

Cheerfulness keeps up a kind of
daylight in the mind, and fills it
with a steady and perpetual serenity.

Joseph Addison

282.

Advice is sometimes transmitted
more successfully through
a joke than grave teaching.

Baltasar Gracián

283.

A good laugh makes us better friends
with ourselves and everybody around us.

Orison Swett Marden

284.

Humor is the great thing, the saving
thing. The minute it crops up all our
irritations and resentments slip away
and a sunny spirit takes their place.

Mark Twain

285.

A smile is a curve
that helps to set things straight.

286.

Cheerfulness: the habit of looking
at the good side of things.

William Ulanthorne

287.

If you can learn to laugh in spite of
the circumstances that surround you,
you will enrich others, enrich yourself,
and, more than that, you will last!

Barbara Johnson

288.

Laughter is a tranquilizer
with no side effects.

289.

Laughter is inner jogging.

Norman Cousins

290.

A cheerful heart is good medicine,
but a crushed spirit dries up the bones.

Proverbs 17:22

291.

Anyone who takes himself too
seriously always runs the risk of
looking ridiculous; anyone who can
consistently laugh at himself does not.

Vaclav Havel

292.

Laughter is the shortest distance
between two people.

Victor Borge

293.

Our mouths were filled with laughter,
our tongues with songs of joy.
Then it was said among the nations,
the Lord has done great things for them.

Psalm 126:2

294.

A good laugh is sunshine in a house.

William Makepeace Thackeray

Communication

295.

Today's kids desperately need dads
who listen eye to eye and with both ears
if it means getting down on one knee.

Marty Wilkins

296.

The more a child becomes aware of
a father's willingness to listen, the
more a father will begin to hear.

Gordon MacDonald

297.

The most important thing in communication
is to hear what isn't being said.

Peter F. Drucker

298.

Communication means a sharing
together of what you really are. With
the stethoscope of love you listen until
you hear the heartbeat of the other.

Bartlett and Margaret Hess

299.

My dear brothers, take note of this: Everyone should be quick to listen, slow to speak.

James 1:19

300.

Eye contact is crucial not only in making good communication contact with a child, but also in filling his emotional needs.

Ross Campbell

301.

Many things we need can wait.
The child cannot. Now is the time his bones are being formed; his blood is being made; his mind is being developed. To him we cannot say tomorrow. His name is today.

Gabriela Mistral

302.

The typical parent spends less than one hour per week in meaningful interaction with each of his or her children.

George Barna

303.

There are times when encouragement means such a lot. And a word is enough to convey it.

Grace Sticker Dawson

304.

Kind words are jewels that live in the heart and soul and remain as blessed memories years after they have been spoken.

Marvea Johnson

305.

Hearing is one of the body's five senses. But listening is an art.

Frank Tyger

306.

To observe people in conflict is a necessary part of a child's education. It helps him to understand and accept his own occasional hostilities and to realize that differing opinions need not imply an absence of love.

Milton Sapirstein

307.

You can never establish a personal relationship
without opening up your own heart.

Paul Tournier

308.

Rash language cuts and maims,
but there is healing in the words of the wise.

Proverbs 12:18 THE MESSAGE

309.

No dreamer is ever too small;
no dream is ever too big.

310.

If your foot slips, you may recover your
balance, but if your tongue slips,
you cannot recall your words.

Martin Vanbee

311.

Kind words heal and help;
cutting words wound and maim.

Proverbs 15:4 THE MESSAGE

312.

Conversation means being able to disagree
and still continue the conversation.

Dwight MacDonald

313.

Bedtime is a good time for heart-to-heart chats
because children share more freely when they are
relaxed, and have nothing else to distract them.

314.

A wise man will hear, and will increase
learning; and a man of understanding
shall attain unto wise counsels.

Proverbs 1:5 KJV

315.

I've learned that you can't expect children to
listen to your advice and ignore your example.

316.

Words kill, words give life;
they're either poison or fruit – you choose.

Proverbs 18:21 THE MESSAGE

317.

Real communication
is impossible without listening.

Ralph C. Smedley

318.

Speak not injurious words,
neither in jest nor earnest;
scoff at none although they give occasion.

George Washington

319.

The real art of conversation is not only to say the
right thing at the right place but to leave unsaid
the wrong thing at the tempting moment.

Dorothy Nevill

Helping Kids
to Live Well

320.

We want our children to grow up to be such
persons that ill-fortune, if they meet with it, will
bring out strength in them, and that good fortune
will not trip them up, but make them winners.

Edward Sandford Martin

321.

The best and noblest lives are those which
are set toward high ideals.

René Alemeras

322.

One is happy once one knows the necessary
ingredients of happiness – simple tastes, a certain
degree of courage, self-denial to a point, love of
work, and above all, a clear conscience. Let us
live life as it is, and not be ungrateful.

George Sand

323.

Heads are wisest when they are cool,
and hearts are strongest when they
beat in response to noble ideals.

Ralph Bunche

324.

O Divine Master, grant that we may not so
much seek to be consoled as to console, not so
much to be understood as to understand, not
so much to be loved as to love.

St. Francis of Assisi

325.

This is the only chance you will ever have
on this earth with this exciting adventure
called Life. So why not plan it, and try to
live it as richly and as happily as possible?

Dale Carnegie

326.

The vision that you glorify in your mind, the
ideal that you enthrone in your heart – this you
will build your life by, this you will become.

James Allen

327.

The great thing in the world
is not so much where we are,
but in what direction we are moving.

Oliver Wendell Holmes

328.

What a large volume of adventures
may be grasped within the little span of life,
by him who interests his heart in everything,
and who, having eyes to see what time and
chance are perpetually holding out to him
as he journeyeth on his way, misses
nothing he can fairly lay his hands on!

Laurence Stern

329.

Excellence is best described
as doing the right things right – selecting the
most important things to be done and then
accomplishing them 100% correctly.

330.

Resolved: to live with all might while I do live.

Jonathan Edwards

331.

"The thief comes only to steal and kill and destroy; I have come that they may have life, and have it to the full."

John 10:10

332.

Undertake something that is difficult; it will do you good. Unless you try to do something beyond what you have already mastered, you will never grow.

Ronald E. Osborn

333.

We live, and we learn, as much by unconscious absorption and imitation as by systematic effort.

Luella Cook

334.

Sons are a heritage from the LORD, children a reward from Him. Like arrows in the hands of a warrior are sons born in one's youth.
Blessed is the man whose quiver is full of them.

Psalm 127:3-5

335.

Nothing gives one person so much
advantage over another as to remain cool
and unruffled under all circumstances.

Thomas Jefferson

336.

A successful house anywhere
is one where you sense immediately
that the people who live in it are
really involved in being alive.

Benjamin Franklin

337.

A wise son brings joy to his father,
but a foolish son grief to his mother.

Proverbs 10:1

338.

What is there to do with life
but live it to the full?

Arnold Glasow

339.

No man knows his true character until he
has run out of gas, purchased something on the
installment plan and raised an adolescent.

Marcelene Cox

340.

Re raising children: Trust yourself.
You know more than you think you do.

Benjamin Spock

341.

Adolescence is like a house on moving
day – a temporary mess.

Julius Warren

342.

What is best for people is
what they do for themselves.

Benjamin Franklin

343.

You cannot teach a [child] anything.
You can only help him discover it within himself.

Galileo Galilei

344.

Let's not waste a second worrying because
we are not like other people. You are something
new in this world. Never before, since
the beginning of time, has there ever been
anybody exactly like you; and never again
throughout all the ages to come will there
ever be anyone exactly like you again.

Dale Carnegie

345.

A young man should look for the single
spark of individuality that makes him
different from other folks, and develop
that for all its worth. Don't let that spark be lost.

Henry Ford

346.

The man who graduates today and stops learning tomorrow is uneducated the day after.

Newton D. Baker

347.

One must have the adventurous daring to accept oneself as a bundle of possibilities and undertake the most interesting game in the world – making the most of one's best.

Henry Fosdick

348.

The confidence which we have in ourselves gives birth to much of that which we have in others.

Francois de la Rochefoucauld

349.

God is the first object of our lives
Its next office is to bear the defects of others. And we should begin the practice of this amid our own household.

John Wesley

350.

Be glad of life because it gives you
the chance to love and to work
and to play and to look up at the stars.

Henry van Dyke

351.

That is what every successful man loves:
the game. The chance for self-expression.
The chance to prove his worth, to excel, to win.

Dale Carnegie

352.

Be hard on standards, but soft on your teenager.

Arnold Mol

353.

The boy who is going to make a great man,
or is going to count in any way in later life,
must make up his mind not merely to
overcome a thousand obstacles, but to win in
spite of a thousand repulses and defeats.

Theodore Roosevelt

354.

Wise fathers know that their worth does not lie in the things they do for their children, but in what they teach their children to do by themselves.

Billy Graham

355.

The very first step toward success in any occupation is to become interested in it.

Dale Carnegie

356.

When a man dies, if he can pass enthusiasm along to his children, he has left them an estate of incalculable value.

Thomas Edison

357.

I've learned that parenthood is the most responsible job anyone can fill.

Leo Buscaglia

358.

The grandest of heroic deeds are those
which are performed within four walls
and in domestic privacy.

Jean Paul Richter

359.

To improve the golden moments of
opportunity and catch the good that is
within our reach, is the great art of living.

Samuel Johnson

360.

The father of a righteous man has great joy; he
who has a wise son delights in him. May your
father and mother be glad; may she who gave
you birth rejoice! My son, give me your heart and
let your eyes keep to my ways.

Proverbs 23:24-26

361.

When a man begins to understand himself
he begins to live. When he begins
to live he begins to understand his fellow men.

Norvin McGranahan

362.

The future belongs to those who believe
in the beauty of their dreams.

Eleanor Roosevelt

363.

Let love and faithfulness never leave you; bind
them around your neck, write them on the tablet
of your heart. Then you will win favor and a
good name in the sight of God and man.

Proverbs 3:3-4

364.

God created us with an overwhelming
desire to soar ... He designed us to be
tremendously productive and "to mount
up with wings like eagles," realistically dreaming
of what He can do with our potential.

Carol Kent

365.

Let your children go
if you want to keep them.

Malcolm Forbes